MW00957889

Military Motorcycles

by Michael Green

Reading Consultant:

Sergeant James Petersen (retired)

United States Air Force

CAPSTONE BOOKS

an imprint of Capstone Press

Mankato, Minnesota

Capstone Books are published by Capstone Press
151 Good Counsel Drive, P.O. Box 669, Mankato, Minnesota 56002
http://www.capstone-press.com

Printed in the United States of America.

Library of Congress Cataloging-in-Publication Data
Green, Michael, 1952–
Military motorcycles/by Michael Green.
p. cm. — (Land and sea (Mankato, Minn.))
Includes bibliographical references and index.
Summary: Discusses the history and use of military motorcycles, highlighting specific models and their roles in various battles.
ISBN 1-56065-462-7
1. Military motorcycles—Juvenile literature. [1. Motorcycles, Military.]
I. Title. II. Series.
UG615.G745 1997
623.7'47—dc21

96-39036
CIP
AC

Photo credits
Dean and Nancy Kleffman: 32, 47
Michael Green: 8
Patton Museum: 6, 10-24
Richard Pemberton: 26, 30, 36
U.S. Army: 4, 34, 38, 41

2 3 4 5 6 05 04 03 02 01

Table of Contents

Features

Pronunciation guides follow difficult words, both in the text and in the Words to Know section in the back of the book.

Chapter 1

Military Motorcycles

The word "motorcycle" combines the words "motor" and "bicycle." A motorcycle is a bicycle with a motor. A military motorcycle is a special kind of motorcycle. It is made to carry soldiers.

Military motorcycles carry soldiers in peacetime and in wartime. They perform many different jobs. Soldiers have found that military motorcycles are especially good for delivering orders when radios break down.

Motorcycle Scouts

Military motorcycles have been used as scout vehicles. Scouts are people who spy on enemy

Military motorcycles were first used as scout vehicles.

troops. Scout vehicles are the machines scouts drive while they are spying.

Motorcycles are good scout vehicles because they are small. With special, quiet mufflers, they can sneak up on the enemy. Motorcycles also are easy to hide. They can go places that other vehicles cannot.

Motorcycle Drawbacks

Military motorcycles are armed with machine guns and mortars. Mortars are small cannons. Some armies have used their motorcycles as attack vehicles.

These military motorcycles are armed with machine guns that the drivers can remove and use.

But without armor, military motorcycles can be easily destroyed by enemy weapons. Armor is anything used to protect vehicles, people, and cargo during combat. Armor is usually made of steel.

Military motorcycles are difficult to operate on wet roads. They slip and slide and can wipe out. They are useless in snow or on ice. The soldiers who drive the motorcycles are exposed to heat and cold. They have a hard job.

BICYCLE MILITARY MEN'S M305 & B
Huffman MFG. Co.
General Data

Chapter 2

The First Military Motorcycles

Armies have always looked for new ways to move around. For a long time, armies used horses. By 1870, some armies began using bicycles.

The invention of small gasoline engines turned the bicycle into the motorcycle. A German inventor built the first practical, working motorcycle in 1885. The German army first used motorcycles in 1904. The German army had more than 5,000 motorcycles in use by 1918.

Armies used bicycles before the motorcycle was invented.

British Army Motorcycles

The British army first used motorcycles in 1914. They had almost 50,000 motorcycles in use by 1919. Most were used only as messenger vehicles.

Some British army motorcycles were equipped with machine guns. The machine guns were mounted on sidecars. Sidecars are wheeled carts attached to one side of a motorcycle.

Many early U.S. Army motorcycles had sidecars.

Some British motorcycles with sidecars were modified into ambulances. Instead of weapons, they carried two stretchers.

U.S. Army Motorcycles

The U.S. Army first used motorcycles during World War I (1914-1918). The army used about 10,000 civilian motorcycles. Civilian means they were not made to be used by the military.

These motorcycles mostly delivered messages. The U.S. Army continued to use motorcycles to deliver messages after the war.

The U.S. Army did not develop special motorcycles for wartime use. They did not have enough money. They were forced to buy civilian motorcycles for military purposes.

Civilian Motorcycles

The civilian motorcycles were designed for highway use only. They were not designed as

Indian was one of the first makers of U.S. military motorcycles.

off-road military vehicles. The motorcycles were unpopular with soldiers. They were heavy, hard to steer, and noisy.

The U.S. Army bought motorcycles from Harley-Davidson and Indian. Both of these motorcycle companies started doing business in the early 1900s. The U.S. Marine Corps

(KOHR) also used Harley-Davidson and Indian motorcycles. Indian went out of business in 1953. Harley-Davidson continues to build motorcycles today.

Scout Motorcycles

In the 1930s, scouts on horses could not keep up with improved army trucks. So the U.S. Army gave each scout a motorcycle. It was

Harley-Davidson made many early U.S. military motorcycles.

called the Model WLA. Motorcycle scouts were supposed to travel faster and farther than scouts on horses.

The new motorcycles were very fast on highways. But they were slower than horses on rough gound. They also broke down a lot.

This early military motorcycle was chain driven.

Scout motorcycles had to be carried in trucks over rough ground.

The Model WLA

The Model WLA was designed and built by Harley-Davidson. The design was based on an older civilian model.

The Model WLA had a chain-driven gasoline engine. Chain driven means that a chain transfers the engine's power to the rear wheel. A bicycle is chain driven.

The Model WLA's top speed was 70 miles (112 kilometers) per hour on the highway. On rough ground, the top speed was 25 miles (40 kilometers) per hour. On a full tank of gas, the Model WLA could travel 124 miles (198 kilometers).

Problems with the Model WLA

The Model WLA had an old-fashioned, hand-operated shift lever. This forced the motorcycle operator to take one hand off the handlebars to shift. This was dangerous at high speeds or over rough ground. Many motorcycle operators crashed.

The Model WLA operator wore a holster for a submachine gun. Extra ammunition and hand grenades were carried in leather saddlebags. The army thought soldiers could fire weapons

The U.S. Army decided that the early military motorcycles it had tested were useless.

while driving motorcycles. But tests showed that it was nearly impossible to do both things at once.

The army conducted many tests with the Model WLA. They decided that the motorcycle was useless.

IBLE

Chapter 3

A Replacement for the WLA

The United States entered World War II (1939-1945) in 1941. The U.S. Army decided to try some new motorcycles. They tested two new scout motorcycle designs. Both designs were copies of a captured German army motorcycle.

One model was built by Harley-Davidson. It was known as the XA model. The other model was built by Indian. It was known as the Model 841.

During World War II, the United States decided to try new motorcycles that were copies of German motorcycles.

Harley-Davidson built this Model XA.

New Features

Both models had foot-operated shift levers. Motorcycle operators did not have to take their hands off the handlebars. This was much safer. Foot-operated shift levers are standard on most motorcycles today.

These new models also had shaft-driven engines. At the time, most U.S. motorcycles had chain-driven engines. Exposed chain-driven engines collected dust and dirt. This often caused engine failure. Shaft-driven engines are completely enclosed. No dust or dirt can enter the engine compartment.

The army ordered 1,000 motorcycles from both companies. They put the motorcycles through many tests. But the new motorcycles did not impress the U.S. Army. The XA model and the Model 841 were never placed into full-scale production. Most of these motorcycles were later sold to civilians.

Something Better

The U.S. Army had a limited amount of money to spend on vehicles. In 1942, they decided to spend their money on four-wheel-drive vehicles (4x4s). These vehicles could be used in many more ways than motorcycles.

The army developed a light 4x4 nicknamed the Jeep. It proved itself in army tests. The Jeep was everything the motorcycle was not.

The Jeep could carry four soldiers and their gear. It performed well on rough ground. It was

This is one of the many Harley-Davidson military motorcycles used during World War II.

lightweight and quiet. Soldiers could fire their weapons while the Jeep was moving.

U.S. Motorcycles at War

The U.S. Army only used 5,000 motorcycles during World War II. They used more than 600,000 Jeeps.

Harley-Davidson built 90,000 motorcycles during World War II. Most were given to Allied armies. Allied armies are those that fought on the same side as the United States. The largest users of U.S. motorcycles were Canada and Great Britain. The Russian army was also given large numbers of U.S.-built motorcycles.

SS-122040

Chapter 4

German Military Motorcycles

The German army made several models of military motorcycles during the 1930s. These motorcycles were designed for off-road military operations. They were well made and very dependable.

German companies were making the best motorcycles in the world during the 1930s. U.S. motorcycles of the 1930s were not as good as German models.

German motorcycle units performed well during early training exercises. The German

German military motorcycles are some of the best ever built.

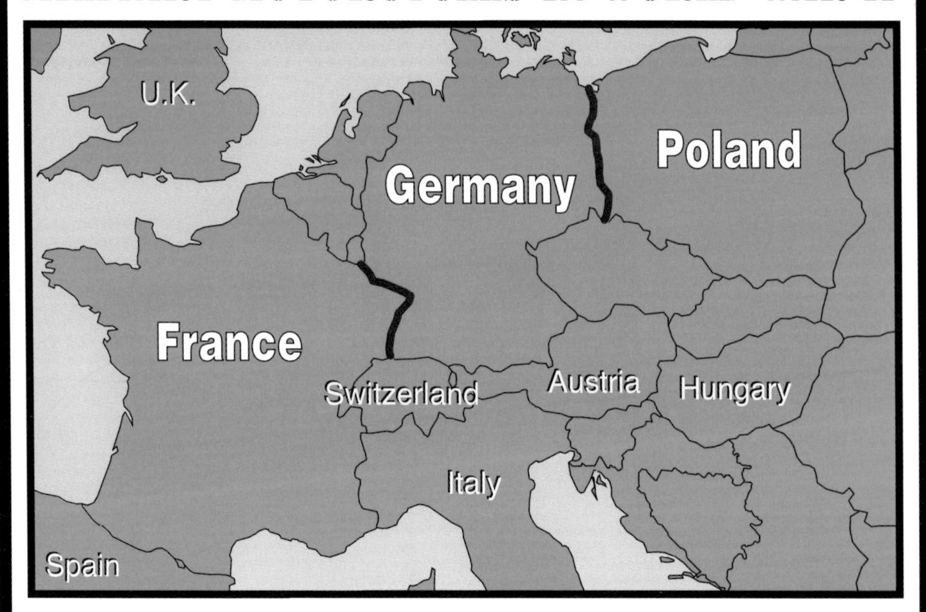

The highlighted border between Germany and Poland is where World War II started. The highlighted border between Germany and France is where the German motorcycles led the forces that invaded France.

army decided that entire ground units would be given motorcycles. German army units were forced to give up their horses. They were then given motorcycles.

Motorcycles with Sidecars

The German army had many motorcycles with sidecars. These huge machines were eight feet (two and one-half meters) long and five feet (one and one-half meters) wide. They could carry three soldiers and their weapons. They weighed close to 900 pounds (405 kilograms).

German Motorcycles at War

German motorcycle units led the attack on Poland in 1939. This attack was the beginning of World War II. German motorcycle units raced across the Polish border. They captured bridges, important river crossings, and even small towns.

German motorcycle units also led the attack on France in 1941. German motorcyclists cruised ahead of their tank units. Tanks are enclosed vehicles protected with heavy armor. Tanks are mounted with various weapons, one of which is usually a large cannon.

The French soldiers fired at the German motorcycle units. The German motorcyclists

German military motorcycles with sidecars had three-man crews.

took cover. Some of the German soldiers returned the French fire. Others sped away to tell the waiting troops and tanks of the enemy's position. Tanks came forward to support the motorcyclists.

The German tanks destroyed the French defenders. The German motorcyclists were sent

forward again to lead the next advance. The German army conquered France in five weeks.

The Last of the Motorcycles

The German army invaded Russia in June 1941. The bad roads in Russia were hard on German motorcycles. Many motorcycles had major mechanical problems and were left behind. The harsh Russian winter finished off the rest of the German motorcycle fleet.

In 1942, the Germans replaced some of their motorcycles with a small, light car. It was known as the Volkswagen Type 82. It had an air-cooled engine. Air-cooled engines need less maintenance than water-cooled engines. But they can overheat faster. The Volkswagen had better off-road abilities than any motorcycle.

Tracked Motorcycles

Motorcycles are useless in too much mud and snow. So the Germans built a tracked motorcycle. Tracks are metal belts that run

German tracked motorcycles combined the features of both motorcycles and tanks.

around wheels on both sides of a vehicle. The front half of the German vehicle was like a motorcycle. The rear half had tracks like a tank.

The tracked motorcycle had a water-cooled engine. It could carry a driver and two passengers. The vehicle had a top speed of 50 miles (80 kilometers) per hour. It could tow a small trailer.

Chapter 5

Safety Problems

Most armies lost interest in motorcycles after World War II. But a lot of former soldiers still liked them. They had developed an interest in motorcycles during the war.

Motorcycle racing became popular in Europe and the United States. Off-road motorcycle designs improved. In the 1960s, light, reliable motorcycles were developed.

These new motorcycles were much better than earlier models. Motorcycle builders had spent the time and money to make them better.

Motorcycles developed since the 1960s are much improved.

Spare Tire
Sidecar
Saddlebags

World War II
German Military Motorcycle
Front Brake
WH 65 618
Shock Absorber

The U.S. Army tested the improved motorcyles.

Their efforts produced good, inexpensive motorcycles.

The U.S. Army Shows Interest Again

In the 1970s, the U.S. Army looked at the new motorcycles. The army wanted to use them as scout vehicles. They conducted several tests.

The first test was performed in 1972. Several off-road civilian motorcycles were used in the tests. The army found that scouts on motorcycles could be effective.

Motorcycle scouts performed missions faster than scouts on foot. The motorcycles were light enough to be carried in helicopters. They could also be carried by ground vehicles.

Safety Problems Reappear

U.S. Army tests showed that motorcycle scouts still had problems. Motorcyclists could not defend themselves if they ran into enemy soldiers. Scouts would be killed by the time they could lay down their motorcycles and pull out their weapons.

The tests also showed that the motorcycles were still dangerous to operate. The motorcycles could not be used on slick or icy roads. Motorcyclists had no protection in cold or rainy weather.

Dead End for Military Motorcycles

The U.S. Army was disappointed with the new off-road motorcycles. The army came to the same conclusion they had come to in the early 1940s. The motorcycles offered no advantages over 4x4 vehicles. The army decided not to buy any of the motorcycles.

But the U.S. Army's lack of interest in motorcycles may not last forever. Many armies around the world use motorcycles in large numbers. New kinds of motorcycles might still be developed. They might have advantages the U.S. Army can use.

The Hummer

Today, instead of military motorcycles, the U.S. Army uses a 4x4 vehicle called the Hummer. The Hummer replaced the Jeep, which was one of the most popular military vehicles ever. Like the Jeep, the Hummer can be bought in a special version for civilian use.

The U.S. Army liked the improved motorcycles, but did not think they had any advantages over 4x4 vehicles.

Words to Know

armor (AR-mur)—anything used to protect vehicles, people, and cargo during combat

chain drive (CHAYN DRIVE)—a system that uses a chain to transfer the engine's power to the rear wheel

civilian (si-VIL-yuhn)—anything not intended for use by the military

hand grenade (HAND gruh-NADE)—a small bomb that is thrown by hand or fired from a launcher

Harley-Davidson (HAR-lee DAY-vid-suhn)—the oldest motorcycle manufacturing company in the world; maker of some of the first U.S. military motorcycles

Indian (IN-dee-uhn)—one of the first motorcycle manufacturing companies in the United States; maker of some of the first U.S. military motorcycles; stopped making motorcycles in 1953

Jeep (JEEP)—a small, four-wheel-drive, cross-country military vehicle developed for the U.S. Army in 1940

scout (SKOUT)—person who spies on enemy troops

scout vehicle (SKOUT VEE-uh-kuhl)—the machines scouts drive while they are spying on the enemy

shaft drive (SHAFT DRIVE)—a system that uses an enclosed shaft to transfer the engine's power to the rear wheel

sidecar (SIDE KAR)—wheeled carts attached to one side of a motorcycle

submachine gun (sub-mu-SHEEN GUHN)—a portable, pistol-type machine gun, usually shot from the hip

tank (TANGK)—enclosed vehicle protected with heavy armor

tracks (TRAKS)—metal belts that run around wheels on both sides of a vehicle

To Learn More

Ansell, David. *Military Motorcycles*. London: B. T. Batsford, 1985.

Passaro, John. *The Story of Harley-Davidson*. Spirit of Success. Mankato, Minn.: Smart Apple Media, 1999.

Smith, Jay H. *Humvees and Other Military Vehicles*. Wheels. Minneapolis: Capstone Press, 1995.

Young, Jesse. *Harley-Davidson Motorcycles*. Minneapolis: Capstone Press, 1995.

Useful Addresses

Military Vehicles Preservation Association
P.O. 520378
Independence, MO 64052

Patton Museum of Cavalry and Armor
4554 Fayette Ave.
Fort Knox, KY 40121-0208

U. S. Army Center for Military History
Fort McNair
103 Third Avenue
Washington, DC 20319-5058

U. S. Army Transportation Museum
Building 300 Besson Hall
Fort Eustis, VA 23604-5259

Internet Sites

Harley-Davidson
http://www.harley-davidson.com/co/en/company.asp?bmLocale=en_US

Indian Military Model 841
http://www.motorcycle.com/mo/mcmuseum/i841.html

Indian Motorcycle
http://www.indianmotorcycles.com/

U. S. Army Center of Military History
http://www.army.mil/cmh-pg/default.htm

This is a close-up look at the driver's compartment of a German tracked motorcycle.

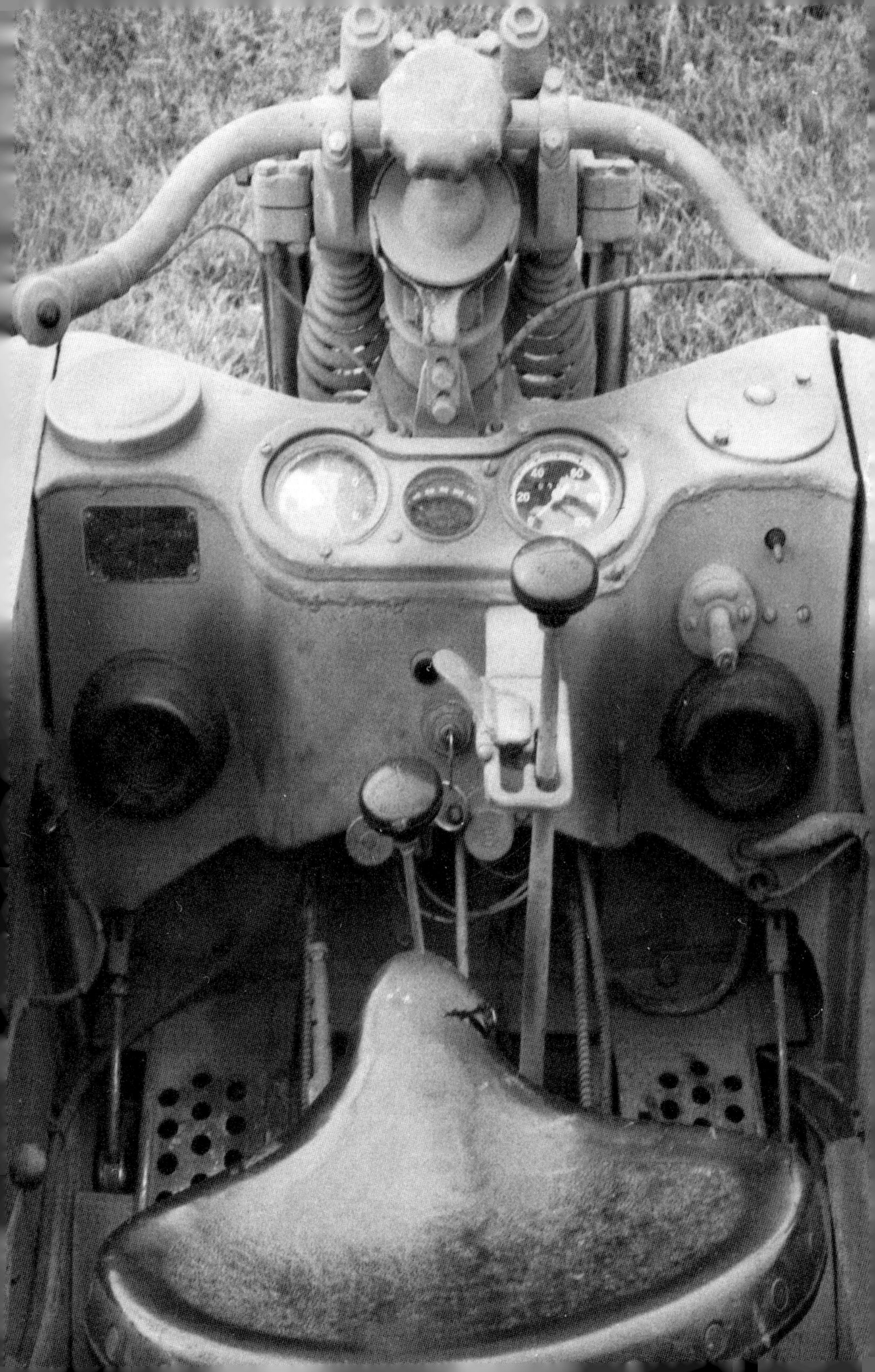

Index